CHILDREN'S ENVIRONMENTS

AMBIENTES PARA NIÑOS

ENVIRONNEMENTS POUR ENFANTS

BEREICHE FÜR KINDER

authors
Fernando de Haro & Omar Fuentes

editorial design & production
AM Editores S.A. de C.V.

project managers
Carlos Herver Díaz
Ana Teresa Vázquez de la Mora
Laura Mijares Castellá

coordination
Emily Keime López
Verónica Velasco Joos
Dulce Ma. Rodríguez Flores

prepress coordination
José Luis de la Rosa Meléndez

copywriters
Gonzalo Ang - Flora Covarrubias Patiño

english translation
Angloamericano de Cuernavaca - Enrique Santiery

french translation
Angloamericano de Cuernavaca - Carmen Chalamanch - Marta Pou

german translation
Angloamericano de Cuernavaca - Sabine Klein

EDITORES   PUBLISHERS

100+ TIPS · IDEAS
children's environments . ambientes para niños
environnements pour enfants . bereiche für kinder

© 2012, Fernando de Haro & Omar Fuentes
AM Editores S.A. de C.V.
Paseo de Tamarindos 400 B, suite 102, Col. Bosques de las Lomas,
C.P. 05120, México, D.F., Tel. 52(55) 5258 0279
ame@ameditores.com / **www.ameditores.com**

ISBN: 978-607-437-221-2

Printed in China.

INTRODUCTION
INTRODUCCIÓN
INTRODUCTION
EINLEITUNG

Creating environments for children's own spaces is not only a matter of decoration, but part of the emotional education that relates to children's moods and visual stimulation, something which stays in their minds for a lifetime. Therefore, particular care has been taken in this book to present a wide range of options for boys' and girls' atmospheres, so that they can be combined to achieve the desired results.

Straight and curved lines, smooth and rough textures, bright and warm areas, brilliant and pastel colors, various shapes and volumes, all come into play when assembling the unique design concept for sons and daughters, where they will study, rest, live and play. A space about them and for them. Safe and endearing. The balanced and stimulating environment to be remembered forever.

However, the design of spaces for the little ones is part of a general concept of the image of the whole house, and the specific environment of their rooms and the children's areas is basically the product of a total family environment. Therefore, the harmony, details and stimuli come from the heart of the parents, and they are reflected in every corner of the home, and can be enjoyed as a family.

Crear el ambiente de los espacios propios para los niños no sólo es un tema de decoración, sino que forma parte de la educación emocional, de los estados de ánimo y de la estimulación visual y plástica de los menores, los cuales permanecerán en su mente durante toda su vida. Por ello, se ha puesto especial cuidado en presentar en este libro una amplia gama de opciones de atmósferas para niños y niñas, con el fin de que puedan combinarse para lograr los resultados esperados.

Líneas rectas y curvas, texturas tersas y rugosas, áreas luminosas y cálidas, colores brillantes y pastel, formas y volúmenes diversos, todo entra en juego a la hora de armar el concepto de diseño único para los hijos e hijas, donde habrán de estudiar, descansar, convivir y jugar. Un espacio de ellos y para ellos. Seguro y entrañable. El ambiente equilibrado y estimulante que habrán de recordar por siempre. Sin embargo, el diseño de los espacios de los pequeños es parte de un concepto general de la imagen de toda la casa, y el ambiente específico de sus habitaciones y de las áreas infantiles es básicamente producto del ambiente familiar total. Por tanto, la armonía, los detalles y los estímulos salen del corazón de los padres y quedan reflejados en cada uno de los rincones del hogar, los cuales podrán disfrutar en familia.

La création d'un environnement approprié aux enfants n'est pas seulement une question de décoration, mais elle fait partie de l'éducation émotionnelle, des états d'âme et de la stimulation visuelle et plastique pour les petits, qui en garderont le souvenir toute leur vie. De ce fait, dans ce livre on a soignée spécialement une large gamme d'atmosphères possibles pour filles et garçons afin de les combiner pour obtenir les résultats attendus.

Lignes droites et courbes, textures lisses et rugueuses, espaces éclairés et accueillants, couleurs brillantes et pastel, formes et volumes divers, tout entre en jeu au moment de créer le concept de design unique pour les enfants, l'environnement où ils vont étudier, se reposer, être ensemble et jouer. Un espace à eux et pour eux. Sûr et cher. L'environnement équilibré et stimulant qui restera toujours dans leur mémoire. Toutefois, le design des espaces pour les petits fait partie d'une conception générale de l'image de toute la maison, et l'ambiance spécifique de leurs chambres à coucher et des espaces consacrés aux enfants est essentiellement le produit de l'environnement familial global. Donc, l'harmonie, les détails et la motivation proviennent du cœur de leurs parents et se reflètent dans chaque coin de la maison, dont ils pourront profiter en famille.

Das Ambiente in den Räumen der Kinder zu schaffen ist nicht nur ein Thema der Dekoration, sondern hat Teil an der Gefühlsentwicklung, der Stimmung und der optischen und plastischen Anregung der Kinder, die sie in ihrem gesamten Leben begleiten wird. Deshalb wird in diesem Buch mit besonderer Sorgfalt eine weite Bandbreite von möglichen Atmosphären für Jungen und Mädchen präsentiert, die kombiniert werden können, um den erwünschten Effekt zu erzielen.

Gerade Linien und Kurven, glatte und raue Texturen, helle und warme Bereiche, leuchtende Farben und Pastelltöne, verschiedenste Formen und Grössen, all dies spielt eine Rolle, wenn es darum geht, ein einzigartiges Designkonzept für die Söhne und Töchter zu entwerfen, in dem sie lernen, ausruhen, Freunde treffen und spielen werden. Ein Raum von ihnen und für sie. Sicher und gemütlich. Ein ausgeglichenes und anregendes Ambiente, das sie niemals vergessen werden.

Allerdings ist das Design der Bereiche für die Kleinen ein Teil des Gesamtkonzeptes des Hauses und die Atmosphäre der einzelnen Zimmer und der Bereiche der Kinder ist grundsätzliche ein Produkt des gesamten familiären Ambientes. Die Harmonie, die Details und die Anregungen kommen aus dem Herzen der Eltern, spiegeln sich in jedem Winkel des Hauses wieder und werden von der ganzen Familie genossen.

GIRLS

NIÑAS

FILLES

MÄDCHEN

The environments created for girls may be dressed up in many ways. But they all seek to fulfill the same purpose: to provide privacy, safety, comfort, harmony and beauty.

For the design of these spaces it is important to consider pastel colors, pinks, reds, lilacs and whites, among others, because, thanks to them, you can create a warm and feminine ambiance.

On the other hand, parents, as well as daughters, may have in mind some basic furniture like the bed, wardrobe, bookcase, work table and chair, shelves and toilet. Other items, such as sofas, toyboxes and drawers are determined by the space available and its arrangement. Also, accessories such as paintings or drawings done by the girls, phrases, lamps, cushions, quilts, curtains, carpets, mirrors, flowers, dolls or vinyls, will give more color, brightness, comfort and sweetness to the girls' bedroom.

Following are some interesting and inspiring samples, not just of bedrooms, but of elegant bathrooms, comfortable lounges and functional work areas.

Los ambientes creados para las niñas pueden estar revestidos de muchos modos. No obstante, todos buscan cumplir el mismo cometido: brindar privacidad, seguridad, comodidad, armonía y belleza.

Para el diseño de estos espacios es importante considerar los colores pasteles, rosados, rojos, lilas y blancos, entre otros, pues gracias a ellos, podrá crearse un ambiente cálido y femenino.

Por otro lado, tanto padres como hijas, pueden tener en cuenta muebles básicos como la cama, el guardarropa, los libreros, la silla y la mesa de trabajo, los anaqueles y el tocador. Otros más, como sofás, jugueteros y cajoneras se determinarán según el espacio disponible y la distribución. Asimismo, accesorios como cuadros o dibujos hechos por las niñas, frases, lámparas, cojines, edredones, cortinas, alfombras, espejos, flores, muñecos o vinilos, darán más colorido, iluminación, comodidad y dulzura a la recámara de las niñas.

A continuación, se presentan algunas muestras interesantes e inspiradoras, no sólo de dormitorios, sino de elegantes baños, confortables salas de descanso y funcionales áreas de trabajo.

Les environnements consacrés aux petites filles peuvent être revêtus de différentes manières. Toutefois, ils cherchent tous à atteindre le même but : offrir intimité, sécurité, confort, harmonie et beauté.

Pour le design de ces espaces, il est important de penser aux couleurs pastel, roses, rouges, lilas et blanches, entre autres, car grâce à elles on pourra créer un environnement accueillant et féminin.

D'un autre côté, les parents aussi bien que les petites filles peuvent penser aux meubles essentiels, comme le lit, l'armoire, les bibliothèques, la chaise et la table de travail, les étagères et la coiffeuse. Les autres, comme les canapés, les coffres à jouets et les chiffonniers, sont déterminés par l'espace disponible et la distribution. Également, les accessoires comme les tableaux ou les dessins faits par les petites filles, les phrases, les lampes et les coussins, les duvets, rideaux, tapis, miroirs, fleurs, poupées ou les disques apporteront de la couleur, de l'éclairage, du confort et de la douceur à la chambre à coucher des petites filles.

Ci-après, vous trouverez quelques idées intéressantes et inspiratrices, non seulement pour les chambres à coucher, mais aussi pour des salles de bain élégantes, des salles de séjour confortables et des espaces fonctionnels pour travailler.

Mädchenzimmer können in verschiedenster Weise ausgestattet sein. Jedoch wollen alle die gleiche Aufgabe erfüllen: Privatsphäre, Sicherheit, Behaglichkeit, Harmonie und Schönheit zu bieten.

Für das Design dieser Bereiche ist es wichtig, unter anderen, Pastellfarben, Rosa-, Rot-, Lila- und weisse Töne in Betracht zu ziehen, da Dank ihnen ein warmes und weibliches Ambiente geschaffen werden kann.

Andererseits sollten sowohl Eltern als auch Töchter eine Grundausstattung Möbel berücksichtigen, wie ein Bett, einen Schrank, Bücherregale, einen Schreibtisch und einen dazu passenden Stuhl, Regale und einen Frisiertisch. Andere, wie Sofas, Spielzeugmöbel und Kommoden können je nach dem zur Verfügung stehenden Platz ausgesucht werden. Auch die Dekoration mit Bildern und Zeichnungen der Mädchen, Sprüchen, Lampen, Kissen, Überdecken, Vorhängen, Teppichen, Spiegeln, Blumen und Puppen geben dem Mädchenzimmer Farbe, Beleuchtung, Behaglichkeit und Lieblichkeit.

Im Folgenden werden einige interessante und inspirierende Beispiele, nicht nur von Schlafzimmern, sondern auch von eleganten Badezimmern, bequemen Ruhebereichen und funktionellen Arbeitsbereichen, präsentiert.

TIPS - ASTUCES - TIPPS
- *Stars, leaves of clover or flowers in the air: beautiful details that will delight the girls.*
- *Estrellas, tréboles o flores en el aire: hermosos detalles que encantarán a las niñas.*
- *Étoiles, trèfles ou fleurs en l'air : de beaux détails que les petites filles adoreront.*
- *Sterne, Kleeblätter und Blumen in der Luft: wunderschöne Details, die Mädchen begeistern.*

The wooden elements create a sense of unity in this bedroom.

Los elementos en madera generan una sensación de unidad en esta recámara.

Dans cette chambre à coucher, les éléments en bois donnent une impression d'unité.

Die Holzmöbel schaffen den Eindruck von Einheit in diesem Zimmer.

TIPS - ASTUCES - TIPPS

- *Lilac tones and classic furnishings give a feminine look to the room.*
- *Los tonos lilas y los muebles clásicos dan un aspecto femenino a la habitación.*
- *Les tons lilas et les meubles classiques créent une apparence féminine pour la chambre à coucher.*
- *Die Lilatöne und die klassischen Möbel verleihen dem Raum eine weibliche Note.*

You see things and say why? but I dream things and say why not?

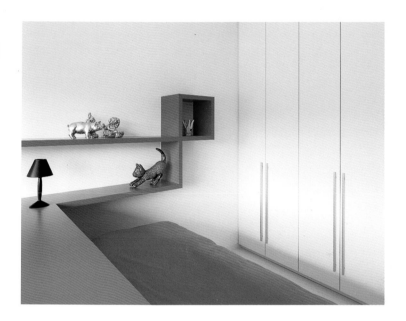

The contrasting colors and lamps accentuate the modern design of these bedrooms.

Los contrastes de color y las lámparas acentúan el moderno diseño de estas recámaras.

Les contrastes de couleur et les lampes accentuent le design moderne de ces chambres à coucher.

Die Farbkontraste und die Lampen betonen das moderne Design dieser Zimmer.

TIPS - ASTUCES - TIPPS
- A phrase on a panel will turn this youngster's room into an endearing atmosphere.
- Una frase sobre un tablero convertirá a esta juvenil habitación en una atmósfera entrañable.
- Une phrase sur un tableau transformera cette chambre jeune en une atmosphère intime.
- Ein Spruch auf einer Platte verleiht diesem jugendlichen Raum eine freundliche Atmosphäre.

TIPS - ASTUCES - TIPPS
- Modular furniture provides storage space and can add colorful accents to the room.
- Los muebles modulares aportan espacio de guardado y pueden agregar notas de color a la habitación.
- Les meubles de différentes couleurs et grandeurs créent une distribution harmonieuse dans un petit espace.
- Modulmöbel liefern Stauraum und können dem Raum Farbakzente geben.

Combining the prints on the bed with the bedroom walls generates a dynamic and energetic effect.

El combinar los estampados de la cama con las paredes del dormitorio genera un efecto dinámico y energético.

La combinaison des imprimés du lit avec les murs de la chambre à coucher crée un effet dynamique et énergétique.

Die Kombination des Musters auf dem Bett mit dem der Wand hat einen dynamischen und energievollen Effekt.

The furniture of different colors and sizes creates a harmonious arrangement in a small space.

Los muebles de distintos colores y tamaños crean una distribución armoniosa en un espacio pequeño.

Les meubles de différentes couleurs et grandeurs créent une distribution harmonieuse dans un petit espace.

Möbel in unterschiedlichen Farben und Grössen schaffen eine harmonische Aufteilung in einem kleinen Raum.

TIPS - ASTUCES - TIPPS
- The elements in pink tones add feminine detail to the girls' bathroom.
- Los elementos en tonos rosados añaden detalles de calidez y feminidad al baño de las niñas.
- Les éléments en tons roses ajoutent des détails de féminité à la salle de bain des filles.
- Die rosafarbenen Stücke sorgen in dem Badezimmer der Mädchen für weibliche Details.

TIPS - ASTUCES - TIPPS
- Using white on the walls and blinds provides a sense of spaciousness to this elegant room.
- El uso del color blanco en muros y persianas brinda una gran sensación de amplitud a esta elegante habitación.
- L'emploi du blanc sur les murs et les stores donne une grande impression d'amplitude à cette élégante chambre à coucher.
- Die Verwendung von weisser Farbe an den Wänden und den Rollos erzeugt den Eindruck von Weite in diesem eleganten Zimmer.

The work and rest areas can be mixed, through the proper arrangement of the furniture.

El área de trabajo puede mezclarse con la de descanso, a través de una distribución correcta del mobiliario.

On peut combiner l'espace de travail et l'espace de repos au moyen d'une distribution correcte du mobilier.

Der Arbeitsbereich und der Ruhebereich können bei geschickter Anordnung der Möbel ineinander übergehen.

In the bathrooms, the use of resistant materials is complemented by a magnificent design.	En los baños, el uso de materiales resistentes se complementa con un magnífico diseño.	Dans les salles de bain, l'emploi de matériaux résistants s'allie à un magnifique design.	In den Bädern wird die Verwendung widerstandsfähiger Materialien von einem grossartigen Design begleitet.

TIPS - ASTUCES - TIPPS
- The smooth textures, soft lighting and white and pastel colors create a relaxing atmosphere.
- Las texturas lisas, la iluminación tenue y los colores blancos y pasteles crean un ambiente relajante.
- Les textures lisses, une illumination douce et les couleurs blanc et pastel créent un environnement délassant.
- Glatte Texturen, eine schwache Beleuchtung und die Weiss- und Pastelltöne schaffen ein entspannendes Ambiente.

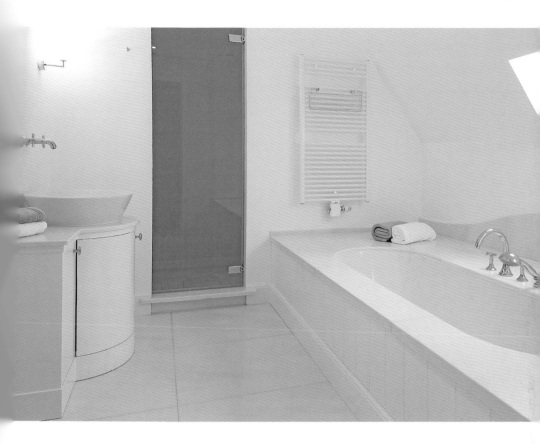

A large mirror creates a feeling of spaciousness in this white bathroom. Between the sinks are beauty products that two girls can share.

Un gran espejo genera una sensación de amplitud a este baño blanco. Entre los lavabos figuran artículos de belleza que dos chicas pueden compartir.

Dans cette salle de bain blanche, un grand miroir produit une impression d'amplitude. Entre les lavabos se trouvent des produits de beauté que deux jeunes filles peuvent partager.

Ein grosser Spiegel verleiht diesem weissen Bad Weite. Zwischen den Waschbecken sind Schönheitsartikel zu sehen, die von den beiden Mädchen geteilt werden.

TIPS - ASTUCES - TIPPS
- *The sets of colorful towels emphasize the total whiteness of the bathroom.*
- *Los juegos de toallas de colores vivos subrayan la blancura total del baño.*
- *Les ensembles de serviettes en couleurs vives mettent en relief la couleur blanche de la salle de bain.*
- *Die Handtücher in lebendigen Farben betonen das vollkommene Weiss des Bades.*

Have fun
Dream, love, fo
To make

The use of different cushions can help create a cozy bedroom.

El uso de cojines distintos puede ayudar a crear una recámara acogedora.

L'emploi de différents coussins peut aider à créer une chambre à coucher accueillante.

Unterschiedlich gemusterte Kissen können helfen ein gemütliches Schlafzimmer zu schaffen.

TIPS - ASTUCES - TIPPS
- The mixture of materials and furniture, modern and retro, make this an original bedroom.
- La mezcla de materiales y muebles, modernos y retro, hacen de éste un dormitorio original.
- Le résultat de la combinaison des matériaux et des meubles, modernes et retro, est une chambre originale.
- Die Mischung aus Materialien und Möbeln, Modern und Retro, machen aus diesem ein originelles Schlafzimmer.

TIPS - ASTUCES - TIPPS
- *The rest area can be defined by a thick rug and youthful sofas.*
- *El área de descanso puede delimitarse con un grueso tapete y juveniles sofás.*
- *L'espace pour le repos peut être délimité par un tapis et des canapés jeunes.*
- *Der Ruhebereich kann durch einen dicken Teppich und jugendliche Sofas abgeteilt werden.*

Color can give unity to the design concept, especially when there is a mix of different prints.

El color permite dar unidad al concepto de diseño, sobre todo cuando hay una mezcla de estampados diferentes.

La couleur permet d'unifier le concept de design, surtout quand il y a un mélange d'imprimés différents.

Die Farbe erlaubt es dem Designkonzept Einheit zu verleihen, vor allem wenn die Muster unterschiedlich sind.

TIPS - ASTUCES - TIPPS

- *The modern design of the arches between the beds and the carpet designs generate a highly dynamic effect.*
- *El moderno diseño de los arcos entre las camas y los dibujos de la alfombra, generan un efecto de gran dinamismo.*
- *Le design moderne des arcs entre les lits et les dessins du tapis produisent un effet de grand dynamisme.*
- *Das moderne Design der Bögen zwischen den Betten und das Muster des Teppichs lassen einen dynamischen Effekt entstehen.*

50

TIPS - ASTUCES - TIPPS
- Placing furniture and objects in pairs provides balance to the bedrooms.
- El disponer muebles y objetos en pares proporciona equilibrio a los dormitorios.
- Placer les meubles et les objets deux par deux crée un équilibre dans les chambres à coucher.
- Möbel und Objekte in Paaren anzuordnen, verleiht Räumen Gleichgewicht.

A study and entertainment area can be created as part of the bedroom.

On peut créer un espace d'étude et de loisir qui fait partie de la chambre à coucher.

Puede crearse una zona de estudio y entretenimiento como parte de la recámara.

Ein Arbeits- und Unterhaltungsbereich kann als Teil des Schlafzimmers eingerichtet werden.

TIPS - ASTUCES - TIPPS
- The large cushions that serve as a headboard give order and elegance to this room.
- Los grandes cojines que sirven de cabecera, dan orden y elegancia a esta recámara.
- Les grands coussins qui servent de tête de lit donnent de l'ordre et de l'élégance à cette chambre à coucher.
- Die grossen Kissen, die als Kopfstück dienen, verleihen dem Raum Ordnung und Eleganz.

A functional study area for doing homework can be arranged within the room.

Dentro de la habitación puede disponerse un área de estudio funcional para realizar las tareas escolares.

Dans la chambre on peut disposer un espace d'étude fonctionnel pour faire les devoirs scolaires.

Im Zimmer kann man einen funktionellen Arbeitsbereich einrichten, in dem die Hausaufgaben gemacht werden können.

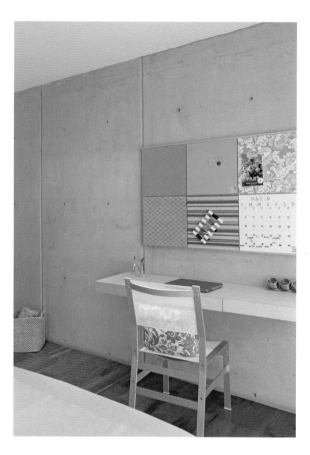

The use of different textures produces a cutting edge concept in this spacious bedroom.

El empleo de diferentes texturas genera un concepto vanguardista en este espacioso dormitorio.

L'emploi de différentes textures génère un concept d'avant-garde dans cette spacieuse chambre à coucher.

Die Verwendung von unterschiedlichen Texturenschafft ein avantgardistisches Konzeptin diesem weiträumigen Schlafzimmer.

TIPS - ASTUCES - TIPPS

- *A strong color like yellow gives life to a traditional color scheme.*
- *Un color fuerte como el amarillo le da vida a un esquema cromático tradicional.*
- *Une couleur intense comme le jaune donne de la vitalité à un schéma chromatique traditionnel.*
- *Eine kräftige Farbe, wie das Gelb, verleiht einem traditionellen Farbschema Leben.*

TIPS - ASTUCES - TIPPS
- *A proper arrangement of furniture and good lighting create a peaceful atmosphere.*
- *Una adecuada disposición de muebles y una buena iluminación crean una atmósfera apacible.*
- *Un arrangement approprié des meubles et un bon éclairage produisent une atmosphère agréable.*
- *Eine angemessene Anordnung der Möbel und eine gute Beleuchtung schaffen eine angenehme Atmosphäre.*

It is desirable that
the study area
be well lit at any
time of day.

Il faut que
l'espace d'étude
soit bien éclairé
à n'importe
quelle heure.

Es conveniente
que la zona
de estudio esté
bien iluminada
a cualquier hora
del día.

Der Arbeitsbereich
sollte zu jeder
Tageszeit gut
beleuchtet sein.

BOYS
NIÑOS
GARÇONS
JUNGEN

Designs for a boy's bedroom are characterized, in principle, by the architectural style and the general concept of the rest of the house. A wide variety of them is suggested in this section. Also taken into account are the child's personality and interests, and the parents' intentions when choosing furniture, decorations and accessories, for both the bedroom and the study area.

A noteworthy point is the designs and textures of the cushions, that are included in virtually all the proposals. Whether they go on the bed, on the sofa or in a chair, cushions are design elements that can give the room its own well defined personality.

Also, in order to maximize the use of space, in a few cases using bunk beds or mezzanines, also called lofts, has been resorted to if the ceiling height allows. From a design standpoint, these options are excellent and enhance the image of the rest of the bedroom.

Los diseños de una recámara para niños están marcados, en principio, por el estilo arquitectónico y por el concepto general del resto de la casa. De ellos se sugiere una amplia variedad, dentro de esta sección. También se toman en cuenta la personalidad del niño y sus intereses, así como la intención de los padres al momento de elegir muebles, adornos y accesorios, tanto para el dormitorio como para el área de estudio.

Como punto digno de destacar, están los diseños y las texturas de los cojines que se incluyen prácticamente en todas las propuestas. Sea que vayan sobre la cama, en el sofá o en una silla, los cojines son elementos de diseño que pueden darle al dormitorio una personalidad propia y bien definida.

Asimismo, con el propósito de aprovechar al máximo el espacio, en unos algunos casos se ha recurrido al uso de literas o al de los entrepisos, también llamados tapancos, si así lo permite la altura del techo. Desde el punto de vista de diseño, esas opciones son excelentes y realzan la imagen del resto del dormitorio.

En principe, le design d'une chambre à coucher pour les garçons est marqué par le style architectonique et le concept général de la maison toute entière. Dans cette section on suggère une grande variété. Il faut aussi tenir compte de la personnalité et des intérêts du garçon, ainsi que le but des parents au moment de choisir les meubles, la décoration et les accessoires pour la chambre à coucher et pour l'espace d'étude.

Les points à souligner sont les imprimés et les textures des coussins qui se trouvent dans pratiquement toutes les propositions. Que ce soit sur le lit, le canapé ou la chaise, les coussins sont des éléments de design qui peuvent créer une personnalité propre et bien définie pour la chambre à coucher.

Également, afin de profiter au maximum de l'espace, dans certains cas on a eu recours à l'emploi des lits superposés ou des entresols, si la hauteur du plafond le permet. Du point de vue du design, ces options sont excellentes et renforcent l'image du reste de la chambre à coucher.

Das Design eines Jungenzimmer ist in erster Linie vom architektonischen Stil und dem generellen Konzept des restlichen Hauses geprägt. In diesem Teil werden eine Bandbreite Konzepte vorgeschlagen. Zugleich sollte die Persönlichkeit und die Interessen des Jungen berücksichtigt werden, so wie auch die Ideen der Eltern bei der Auswahl der Möbel und Dekoration, sowohl im Schlaf- als auch im Arbeitsbereich.

Ein erwähnenswerter Punkt sind die Muster und die Texturen der Kissen, die in praktisch allen Vorschlägen zu finden sind. Ob sie auf dem Bett, auf dem Sofa oder einem Stuhl liegen, Kissen sind Elemente im Design, die einem Zimmer eine eigene und klar definierte Persönlichkeit verleihen.

Auch wurde, um den Raum optimal auszunutzen, in einigen Räumen, in denen die Höhe der Decke es erlaubte, auf Etagenbetten oder Hochbetten zurückgegriffen. Aus der Perspektive des Designs sind sie hervorragende Lösungen, die den Stil des restlichen Raumes betonen.

TIPS - ASTUCES - TIPPS
- Colored stripes often give the decor a jovial effect.
- Las franjas de colores suelen dar a la decoración un efecto de vivacidad.
- Souvent les bandes en couleurs donnent à la décoration un effet de jeunesse.
- Farbige Streifen haben in der Dekoration einen aufheiternden Effekt.

The elements in different materials and textures lend a touch of sophistication to this lively bedroom.

Los elementos en distintos materiales y texturas, dan un toque de sofisticación a este juvenil dormitorio.

Les éléments en différents matériaux et textures apportent une touche de sophistication à cette chambre pleine de vie.

Die Elemente aus verschiedenen Materialien und mit unterschiedlichen Texturen geben diesem lebendigen Raum eine raffinierte Note.

It is essential that the youngster actively participate in the selection of accessories and decorations to be placed in his bedroom.	Es fundamental que los jóvenes participen activamente en la selección de los accesorios y adornos que se coloquen en su recámara.	Il est essentiel que les jeunes participent activement au choix des accessoires et de la décoration de leur chambre à coucher.	Es ist fundamental, dass die jungen Leute aktiv an der Auswahl der Dekorationsstücke, die in ihrem Zimmer Platz finden, teilhaben.

TIPS · ASTUCES · TIPPS
• The room can be well used with a proper distribution of furniture and objects.
• El espacio puede ser muy bien aprovechado con una distribución correcta de muebles y objetos.
• L'espace peut bien être profité avec une bonne distribution de meubles et d'objets.
• Mit einer richtigen Verteilung von Möbeln und Objekten kann der Raum sehr gut verwendet warden.

The use of bunk beds produces more space and comfort for the boys.

El uso de literas genera mayor espacio y mayor comodidad para los niños.

L'emploi de lits superposés donne plus d'espace et de confort pour les enfants.

Etagenbetten schaffen mehr Platz und Nutzmöglichkeiten für die Kinder.

TIPS - ASTUCES - TIPPS
- The bedding and cushions can be combined to give unity to the bedroom.
- Pueden combinarse la ropa de cama y los cojines, para dar unidad al dormitorio.
- Le linge de lit peut être combiné avec les coussins pour créer de l'unité dans la chambre.
- Kombiniert man die Bettdecke mit den Kissen verleiht das dem Raum Einheit.

The white walls combined with vivid colors create brightness and contrast in the bathroom.

Las paredes blancas combinadas con colores vivos generan brillo y contraste en el baño.

Dans la salle de bain, les murs blancs combinés avec des couleurs vives créent luminosité et contraste.

Weisse Wände mit lebendigen Farben kombiniert, bringen Glanz und Kontraste ins Badezimmer.

TIPS - ASTUCES - TIPPS
- The use of wood for the bed, floors and ceilings adds a touch of classic elegance.
- El uso de madera en cama, pisos y techos da un toque de clásica elegancia.
- L'emploi du bois pour le lit, les planchers et les plafonds donne une touche d'élégance classique.
- Holzbetten, Holzböden und –decken verleihen dem Raum eine Note klassischer Eleganz.

TIPS - ASTUCES - TIPPS
- The bedding prints can be matched to the wallpaper stripes.
- El estampado de la ropa de cama puede hacer juego con las rayas del tapiz.
- Les imprimés du linge de lit peuvent répondre au style des rayures du tapis.
- Das Muster auf dem Bettüberwurf passt zu den Streifen des Teppichs.

The brightly colored furniture contrasts with the wood and gray tones.

Los muebles de colores intensos contrastan con la madera y los tonos grises.

Les meubles aux couleurs vives contrastent avec le bois et les tons gris.

Die Möbel in starken Farben stehen im Kontrast zum Holz und den Grautönen.

In addition to
the indirect lighting
in the headboard,
the table lamps
facilitate reading.

Outre les lumières
indirectes de la
tête de lit, les
lampes de bureau
facilitent la lecture.

Además de
las luces indirectas
en la cabecera,
las lámparas de
mesa facilitan la
lectura.

Zusätzlich zu
der indirekten
Beleuchtung
am Kopfende
der Betten
erleichtern die
Nachttischlampen
das Lesen.

Wooden elements make a great contrast with the green of the wall.

Los elementos en madera hacen un magnífico contraste con el verde de la pared.

Les éléments en bois contrastent très bien avec le vert du mur.

Die Holzelemente bilden einen wunderbaren Kontrast zu dem Grün der Wand.

TIPS · ASTUCES · TIPPS
- An integrated modular bed helps store and accomodate toys and other objects.
- Un modular integrado a la cama ayuda a guardar y acomodar juguetes y otros objetos.
- Un modulaire intégré au lit aide à ranger les jouets et autres objets.
- Ein mit dem Bett verbundenes Modul hilft Spielzeug und andere Objekte aufzubewahren.

TIPS - ASTUCES - TIPPS
- Combining textures and vivid colors achieves areas that are very stimulating to look at.
- Al combinar texturas y colores vivos se logran áreas muy estimulantes a la vista.
- En combinant des textures et des couleurs vives on obtient des espaces visuellement très stimulants.
- Mit der Kombination von Texturen und lebendigen Farben erzielt man optisch sehr anregende Bereiche.

The color pattern can be single color, two color or multicolored. The important thing is that it suit the sons' bedroom.

Le schéma chromatique peut être à une seule couleur, deux ou plusieurs. Ce qui compte, c'est qu'il s'adapte à la chambre des enfants.

El patrón cromático puede ser monocolor, bicolor o multicolor. Lo importante, es que éste se adecue al dormitorio de los hijos.

Das Farbschema kann ein-, zwei- oder vielfarbig sein. Wichtig ist, dass es für das Kinderzimmer angemessen ist.

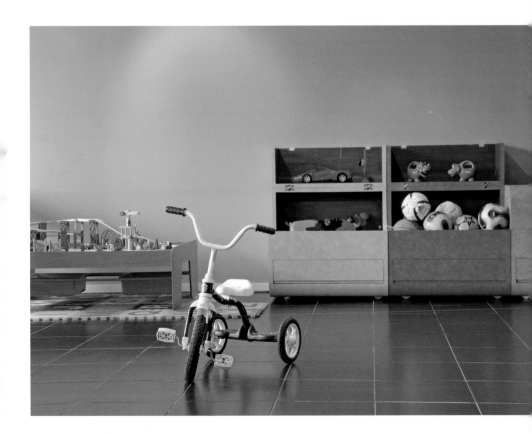

A good color option is to combine the dominant blue of the bedroom with contrasting tones.	Una buena opción de color es combinar el azul dominante del dormitorio con tonos que contrasten.	Une bonne option de couleur est la combinaison du bleu dominant de la chambre avec des tons contrastants.	Eine gute Farboption ist es das im Zimmer dominierende Blau mit kontrastierenden Tönen zu kombinieren.

TIPS - ASTUCES - TIPPS
- Warmth can be added to the bedroom with a fireplace.
- Se puede añadir calidez a la recámara con una chimenea.
- Une cheminée peut rendre la chambre encore plus accueillante.
- Mit einem Kamin kann man dem Schlafzimmer zusätzlich Wärme verleihen.

White color, in different textures, can stand out in its elegance with a single brightly colored accessory.

El color blanco, en diferentes texturas, puede destacar por su elegancia con solo un accesorio de color intenso.

L'élégance de la couleur blanche, en différentes textures, peut être mise en relief avec un seul accessoire de couleur vive.

Weiss, in verschiedenen Texturen, kann wegen seiner Eleganz mit nur einem einzigen Stück in einer intensiven Farbe, betont werden.

In smaller spaces, the use of drawers under the bed, cupboards and wardrobes is recommended.

En espacios reducidos, se recomienda el uso de cajoneras debajo de la cama, armarios y guardarropas.

Dans les espaces réduits, il est conseillé d'employer des chiffonniers sous le lit, des armoires et des garde-robes.

In kleinen Räumen sind Schubladen unter dem Bett, in Schränken und Kleiderschränken zu empfehlen.

TIPS - ASTUCES - TIPPS
- A wall mirror multiplies the light and creates the effect of a larger space.
- Un espejo en la pared multiplica la luz y genera un efecto de mayor espacio.
- Un miroir sur le mur multiplie la lumière et produit l'effet d'un espace plus grand.
- Ein grosser Wandspiegel vervielfältigt das Licht und schafft den Eindruck grösserer Weite.

In double bedrooms, a good option is to arrange the beds in an "L" in order to leave an open space in the center.

Dans les chambres à coucher doubles, l'emplacement des lits en "L" est une bonne option afin de laisser l'espace libre au centre.

En los dormitorios dobles, una buena opción es acomodar las camas en L para dejar un espacio abierto al centro.

Wird das Zimmer geteilt, ist es eine gute Option die Betten in L – Form zu stellen, um die Fläche in der Mitte frei zu lassen.

MIXED

MIXTO

MIXTE

GEMISCHT

In many families designing children's bedrooms (for boys and girls) is unavoidable, especially when they are small, whether because there are three or more children, or because they seek to de-emphasize gender distinctions. This is how mixed bedrooms arise, the following offerings being interesting examples.

Special attention must be paid to color patterns which, not being targeted to the children's genders, are varied and of intense colors and, thus, visually stimulating. These are also areas where different textures, accessories and decorations can be appreciated, but in any case a harmonious and novel effect is obtained, which is positive for child development.

Lighting is a very important factor, so the children can read, play and do their homework in their space. Ideally, there should be sufficient natural light during the day, especially in places where they do their homework. If this is not possible, light colored walls or artificial lighting can compensate.

En muchas familias resulta inevitable diseñar las recámaras de los hijos (niños y niñas), sobre todo cuando son pequeños, ya sea porque hay tres o más hijos o porque no se busca acentuar la distinción de género. Así surgen los dormitorios mixtos, de los que se ofrecen a continuación interesantes muestras.

Especial atención debe ponerse a los patrones cromáticos que, al no estar dirigidos a los menores según su género, resultan variados, de colores intensos y, por tanto, visualmente estimulantes. Asimismo, son espacios donde se aprecian distintas texturas, accesorios y adornos, pero en todos los casos se consigue un efecto armónico y novedoso, positivo para el desarrollo de los menores.

La iluminación es un factor muy importante, pues los niños en su espacio podrán leer, jugar y realizar sus deberes escolares. Lo ideal es contar con suficiente luz natural durante el día, en especial en los sitios donde realizan sus tareas; si esto no es posible, el color claro de las paredes o la liluminación artificial puede compensarla.

Pour de nombreuses familles, il est inévitable de créer des chambres à coucher pour filles et garçons, surtout quand ils sont petits, que ce soit parce que il y a trois enfants ou plus, ou parce qu'on ne désire pas faire une distinction de genres. Ainsi apparaissent les chambres à coucher mixtes, dont nous offrons ci-après des modèles intéressants.

Il faut faire spécialement attention aux schémas chromatiques, car, quand ils ne sont pas dirigés aux enfants selon leur genre, ils peuvent être très variés, en couleurs intenses et donc visuellement stimulants. Ce sont également des espaces où l'on trouve différentes textures, accessoires et décorations, mais dans tous le cas on obtient un effet harmonieux et moderne, positif pour le développement des enfants.

L'éclairage est un facteur très important car dans leur espace les enfants pourront lire, jouer et faire leurs devoirs. Idéalement il devrait y avoir assez de lumière naturelle pendant la journée, notamment à l'endroit où ils font leurs devoirs. Si ceci n'est pas possible, les murs aux couleurs claires ou l'éclairage artificiel peuvent le compenser.

In vielen Familien ist es nicht zu vermeiden die Schlafzimmer der Kinder (Jungen und Mädchen) als gemeinsame Zimmer zu planen, vor allem wenn sie noch klein sind, weil es drei oder mehr Kinder gibt oder weil man sie nicht nach Geschlecht trennen möchte. Von diesen gemischten Schlafzimmern gibt es im folgenden interessante Beispiele.

Besondere Aufmerksamkeit sollte den Farbmustern geschenkt werden, die, da sie nicht auf ein spezifisches Geschlecht gerichtet sind, vielfältig sind, aus kräftigen Farben bestehen und somit optisch anregend wirken. Auch sind dies Räume, in denen verschiedenste Texturen, Zubehör und Dekoration geschätzt werden, aber in denen immer ein harmonischer, neuartiger Effekt erreicht wird, der sich positiv auf die Entwicklung der Kinder auswirkt.

Die Beleuchtung ist ein sehr wichtiger Faktor, da die Kinder in ihrem Raum lesen, spielen und ihre Hausaufgaben machen können müssen. Ideal ist ausreichendes natürliches Licht am Tag, insbesondere in den Bereichen, in denen sie die Hausaufgaben machen; wenn das nicht möglich ist, kann man fehlendes Licht durch eine helle Wandfarbe oder künstliche Beleuchtung ausgleichen.

TIPS - ASTUCES - TIPPS
- It is advisable to use bright colors and furniture appropriate to the children's ages.
- Es recomendable que se usen colores vivos y muebles adecuados a la edad de los hijos.
- Il est conseillé d'employer des couleurs vives et des meubles adaptés à l'âge des enfants.
- Lebendige Farben und dem Alter der Kinder angemessene Möbel sind zu empfehlen.

Places to store
the kids' toys are
always needed.
A good option is
to use paper bags
placed in open
cabinets.

Siempre hacen
falta lugares para
guardar los juguetes
de los chicos. Una
buena opción es
usar bolsas de
papel colocadas en
cajoneras abiertas.

Il faut toujours
des espaces pour
ranger les jouets
des enfants.
Les sacs en papier
dans les chiffonniers
ouverts sont une
bonne option.

Immer fehlt Platz,
um das Spielzeug
der Kinder
unterzubringen.
Eine gute Option ist
es Papierkästen in
offenen Fächern zu
verwenden.

The demarcation of spaces for rest, fellowship and study facilitates orderliness housekeeping in this room.

La délimitation des espaces pour le repos, les amis et l'étude facilite l'ordre et le nettoyage de cette chambre.

La delimitación de los espacios para descanso, convivencia y estudio, facilita el orden y la limpieza en esta habitación.

Die Abgrenzung der Ruhe-, Spiel- und Arbeitsbereiche schafft Ordnung und Sauberkeit in diesem Raum.

Artificial lighting and wood give a special glow to this bedroom.

La iluminación artificial y la madera dan un brillo especial a este dormitorio.

L'éclairage artificiel et le bois donnent une luminosité spéciale à cette chambre à coucher.

Die künstliche Beleuchtung und das Holz geben diesem Zimmer einen besonderen Glanz.

TIPS - ASTUCES - TIPPS
- *Using the elegance of a black wall, the symmetrical elements are framed in this bedroom.*
- *Utilizando a elegancia del negro en la pared, se enmarcan los elementos simétricos de esta recámara.*
- *Les éléments symétriques de cette chambre à coucher sont encadrés par l'élégance du noir pour le mur.*
- *Die schwarze Wand umrahmt mit ihrer Eleganz die symmetrischen Elemente dieses Zimmers.*

The wood floors, in combination with the rugs and blinds, create an atmosphere of warmth in the room.

Los pisos de madera en combinación con los tapetes y persianas, generan un ambiente de calidez en la habitación.

Dans cette chambre, le plancher en bois combiné avec les tapis et les stores produit un environnement accueillant.

Die Holzböden in Kombination mit den Teppichen und Jalousien, lassen in diesem Zimmer ein warmes Ambiente entstehen.

TIPS - ASTUCES - TIPPS
- The sense of order and cleanliness can be maintained with hidden bunk beds in a white bedroom.
- La sensación de orden y limpieza, puede mantenerse con literas ocultas en un dormitorio blanco.
- On peut maintenir la sensation d'ordre et propreté avec des lits superposés dissimulés dans une chambre à coucher blanche.
- Der Eindruck von Ordnung und Sauberkeit kann mit in der Wand eingebauten Etagenbetten in einem weissen Zimmer aufrechterhalten werden.

The prized outdoor view - a lush garden - allows its integration into the interior decor, day and night.

La privilegiada vista exterior - un exuberante jardín - permite integrarlo a la decoración interior, de día y de noche.

La vue privilégiée de l'extérieur - un jardin exubérant - permet de l'intégrer à la décoration intérieure pendant le jour et la nuit.

Die einmalige Aussicht auf einen üppigen Garten lässt sich in die Dekoration, am Tag wie auch in der Nacht, integrieren.

TIPS - ASTUCES - TIPPS

- It is advisable to choose little furniture and few accessories, to keep the children's bedroom clean and tidy.
- Es recomendable elegir pocos muebles y accesorios, para mantener limpio y ordenado el dormitorio de los niños.
- Il est conseillé de choisir peu de meubles et d'accessoires afin de garder la chambre à coucher des enfants propre et ordonnée.
- Es empfiehlt sich nur wenige Möbel und Dekoration zu wählen, um das Kinderzimmer sauber und ordentlich halten zu können.

TIPS - ASTUCES - TIPPS
- Certain objects make each child feel like it is their own bedroom, even though they share it.
- Ciertos objetos hacen que cada niño sienta como propia su recámara, aunque la comparta.
- Certains objets font que l'enfant sente comme sienne la chambre à coucher même s'il la partage.
- Persönliche Objekte lassen jedes Kind das Zimmer als seins empfinden, obwohl es geteilt wird.

A rectangular window is the focal point of this white minimalist bedroom.

Un ventanal rectangular es el punto focal de esta recámara blanca minimalista.

Une grande fenêtre rectangulaire est le point focal de cette chambre à coucher minimaliste blanche.

Ein grosses Wandfenster ist der Blickfang in diesem weissen, minimalistischen Zimmer.

TIPS · ASTUCES · TIPPS
- For aesthetic reasons, it is advised that the central spaces of a shared bedroom be open.
- Por cuestión estética, se aconseja que los espacios centrales de una recámara múltiple sean abiertos.
- Pour une question d'esthétique, il est conseillé de laisser ouverts les espaces du centre de la chambre à coucher multiple.
- Aus ästhetischen Gründen sollten von mehreren Kindern geteilte Zimmer in der Mitte frei gehalten werden.

TIPS - ASTUCES - TIPPS
- *It is important to let the kids apply their personal touch to their bedroom, with elements that distinguish it.*
- *Es importante dejar que los hijos impriman su toque personal a su dormitorio, con elementos que lo distingan.*
- *Il est important de laisser que les enfants impriment leur touche personnelle à leur chambre à coucher avec des éléments qui les distinguent.*
- *Die Kinder sollten die Möglichkeit haben, das Zimmer mit Elementen ihres persönlichen Geschmacks zu prägen.*

The L-shaped wall harmoniously integrates the headboard and bookcases of this modern bedroom.

La pared en L integra armoniosamente la cabecera y libreros de esta moderna recámara.

Le mur en "L" intègre de manière harmonieuse la tête de lit et les bibliothèques de cette chambre moderne.

Die L-förmige Wand integriert harmonisch das Kopfstück des Bettes mit dem Bücherregal in diesem modernen Zimmer.

architecture   arquitectónicos   architectoniques   architektonische

3 MARIANGEL COGHLAN, mariangel coghlan

4-5 VICTORIA PLASENCIA INTERIORISMO,

victoria plasencia

6-7 JS°, javier sánchez

8 (center) BRACHET PROJECT MANAGEMENT,

yvan brachet, (bottom) DUPUIS, alejandra prieto,

cecilia prieto

10 ARCHETONIC, jacobo micha mizrahi

17 MARIANGEL COGHLAN, mariangel coghlan

20-21 MARIANGEL COGHLAN, mariangel coghlan

24-25 NOGAL ARQUITECTOS, josé nogal moragues

26-27 VICTORIA PLASENCIA INTERIORISMO,

victoria plasencia

30 MARIANGEL COGHLAN, mariangel coghlan

34-35 CDS C-CHIC, olga mussali, sara mizrahi

37 (bottom) ARCO ARQUITECTURA

CONTEMPORÁNEA, josé lew kirsch,

bernardo lew kirsch

42-43 VICTORIA PLASENCIA INTERIORISMO,

victoria plasencia

44 MURO ROJO ARQUITECTURA,

elizabeth gómez coello, jorge medina

46-47 COVILHA, blanca gonzález,

maribel gonzález, mely gonzález

48-49 DIN INTERIORISMO, aurelio vázquez

50 MARQCÓ, covadonga hernández

51 (top) ARCO ARQUITECTURA CONTEMPORÁNEA,

josé lew kirsch, bernardo lew kirsch, (bottom)

MARQCÓ, covadonga hernández

52-53 MARQCÓ, covadonga hernández

54-57 a-001 TALLER DE ARQUITECTURA,

eduardo gorozpe fernández

58-59 MARIANGEL COGHLAN, mariangel coghlan

61 (top) VICTORIA PLASENCIA INTERIORISMO,

victoria plasencia

68-69 CDS C-CHIC, olga mussali, sara mizrahi

70-71 GRUPO MM

73 MARQCÓ, covadonga hernández

74-75 ARCO ARQUITECTURA CONTEMPORÁNEA,

josé lew kirsch, bernardo lew kirsch

76 GRUPO ARQUITECTÓNICA, genaro nieto ituarte

78 VICTORIA PLASENCIA INTERIORISMO,

victoria plasencia

79 PASCAL ARQUITECTOS, carlos pascal, gerard pascal

80-81 ECLÉCTICA DISEÑO, mónica hernández sadurní

82-83 MURO ROJO ARQUITECTURA,

elizabeth gómez coello, jorge medina

84-85 GGAD, gerardo garcía

87 DIN INTERIORISMO, aurelio vázquez

88 MARTÍNEZ & SORDO, juan salvador martínez,

luis martín sordo

89 BRACHET PROJECT MANAGEMENT,

yvan brachet

90 ARMELLA ARQUITECTOS, mario armella

91 (bottom) DIN INTERIORISMO, aurelio vázquez

93-95 VICTORIA PLASENCIA INTERIORISMO,

victoria plasencia

100 ECLÉCTICA DISEÑO, mónica hernández sadurní

101 MARIANGEL COGHLAN, mariangel coghlan

102-103 DUPUIS, alejandra prieto, cecilia prieto

107 MARQCÓ, covadonga hernández

110-111 VICTORIA PLASENCIA INTERIORISMO,

victoria plasencia

112-113 DIN INTERIORISMO, aurelio vázquez

114-115 MARIANGEL COGHLAN, mariangel coghlan

121 MARIANGEL COGHLAN, mariangel coghlan

123 ARCHETONIC, jacobo micha mizrahi

126-129 JS°, javier sánchez

130-131 MARTÍNEZ & SORDO, juan salvador

martínez, luis martín sordo

photography   fotográficos   photographiques   fotografische